ENGLISH/POLISH

The T♥ddler's handb◎◎k

with over **100 Words** that every kid should know

BY DAYNA MARTIN

ANGIELSKI/POLSKIE

ENGAGE BOOKS
VANCOUVER

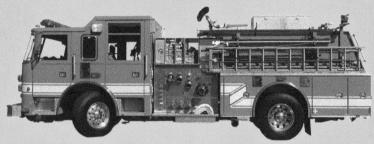

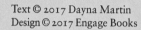

ENGAGE BOOKS

Mailing address
PO BOX 4608
Main Station Terminal
349 West Georgia Street
Vancouver, BC
Canada, V6B 4A1

www.engagebooks.ca

Written & compiled by: Dayna Martin
Edited & translated by: A.R. Roumanis
Proofread by: Karolina Szeląg
Designed by: A.R. Roumanis
Photos supplied by: Shutterstock
Photo on page 47 by: Faye Cornish

FIRST EDITION / FIRST PRINTING

LIBRARY AND ARCHIVES CANADA CATALOGUING IN PUBLICATION

Martin, Dayna, 1983–, author
    The toddler's handbook : numbers, colors, shapes, sizes, ABC animals,
opposites, and sounds, with over 100 words that every kid should know /
written by Dayna Martin ; edited by A.R. Roumanis.

Issued in print and electronic formats.
Text in English and Polish.
ISBN 978-1-77226-468-5 (bound). –
ISBN 978-1-77226-469-2 (paperback). –
ISBN 978-1-77226-470-8 (pdf). –
ISBN 978-1-77226-471-5 (epub). –
ISBN 978-1-77226-472-2 (kindle)

1. Polish language – Vocabulary – Juvenile literature.
2. Vocabulary – Juvenile literature.
3. Word recognition – Juvenile literature.
I. Martin, Dayna, 1983– . Toddler's handbook.
II. Martin, Dayna, 1983– . Toddler's handbook. Polish.
III. Title.

PG6445.M37 2017   J491.8'581   C2017-905772-3
                                             C2017-905773-1

Aa Alligator

Aligator

Bb Bear

4 Niedźwiedź

Cc Cat

Kot

Dog
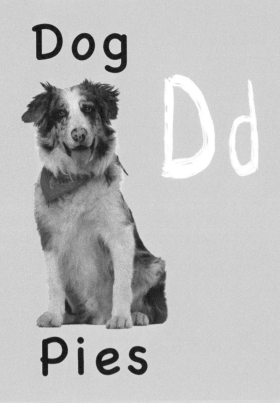
Dd

Pies

Elephant

Ee

Słoń

Fox

Ff

Lis

Goat
Gg

Koza

5

Horse
Hh

Koń

Iguana
Ii

Iguana

Jj
Jaguar

Jaguar

6

Koala

Kk

Koala

Lion

Ll

Lew

Mouse

Mm

Mysz

Newt

Nn

Traszka 7

Otter
Oo

Wydra

Pig
Pp

Świnia

Quail
Qq

8 Przepiórka

Rabbit
Rr

Królik

Seal
S s

Foka

Tiger
T t

Tygrys

Uakari
U u

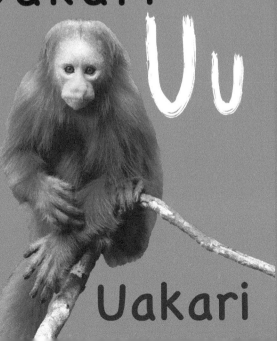

Uakari

Vulture
V v

Sęp

9

Weasel

Ww

Łasica

X-ray fish

Xx

Prystelka

Yak

Yy

10   Jak

Zebra

Zz

Zebra

Apple

One

1

Jedno

Jabłko

Crackers

Two

2

Dwa

Krakersy

Watermelon slices

Three

3

Trzy

Kawałki arbuza

11

Strawberries

Four
4
cztery

Truskawki

Carrots

Five
5
Pięć

Marchewek

Tomatoes

Six
6
Sześć

12

Pomidorów

Pumpkins

Seven

7

Siedem

Dyń

Fruit slices

Eight

8

Osiem

Kawałków
owoców

Potatoes

Nine

9

Dziewięć

Ziemniaków

Cookies

Ten

10

Dziesięć

Ciasteczek 13

Rainbow

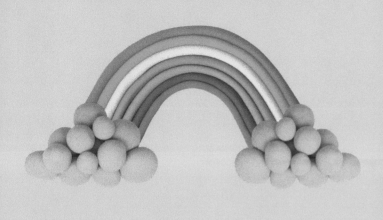

Tęcza

Red

Czerwony

Orange

14 Pomarańczowy

Yellow

Żółty

Green

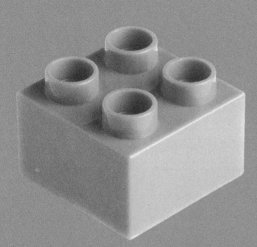

Zielony

Blue

Niebieski

Indigo

Indygo

Violet

Fioletowy

Up
Góra

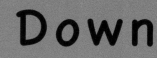

Down

Dół

In

W

Out

Poza

16

Hot
Gorący

Cold
Zimny

Wet
Mokry

Dry
Suchy

Front

Przód

Back

Tył

Turn on

Włączyć

18

Turn off

Wyłączyć

Open
Otwarty

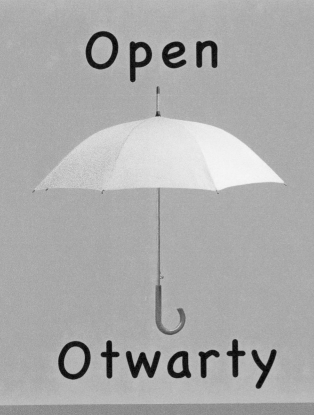

Closed
Zamknięty

Empty

Pusty

Full

Pełny

19

Safe

Dangerous

Bezpieczny

Niebezpieczny

Big

Small

20 Duży

Mały

Asleep

Śpiący

Awake

Rozbudzony

Long

Długi

Short

Krótki 21

Circle

Kółko

Square

Kwadrat

Triangle

Trójkąt

Rectangle

Prostokąt

Diamond

Romb

Star

Gwiazda

Oval

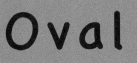

Owal

Heart

Serce

23

Sneeze
Ah-choo

A-psik

Kichać

Duck

Quack

Kwa

Kaczka

Cow

Moo

Muuuu

24 Krowa

Phone
Ring

Dryń

Telefon

Monkey

Ooh-
ooh-
ahh-
ahh

hoo-
hoo-
aah-

Małpa

Frog

Ribbit

Rech

Żaba

Hush

Shh

Ćśśś

Cicho

25

Rooster

cock-a-
doodle-doo

Kukuryku

Kogut

Drums

Boom

Bum

Perkusja

Snake

Hiss

Sssssss

Wąż

26

Owl

Hoot

Hu-huuu

Sowa

Bumblebee

BUZZ

BZZZZZZ

Trzmiel

Hands

Clap

Klaskać

Ręce

Lamb

Baa

Beee

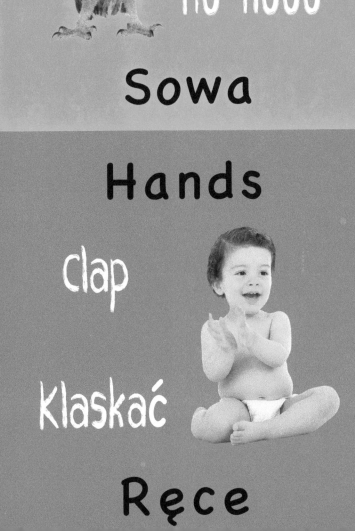

Owieczka 27

Crawl
Czołgać się

Roll
Rolować się

Walk
28 Spacerować

Run
Biegać

Hop

Podskakiwać

Ride

Jeździć

Kiss

Całować

Jump

Skakać

Happy

Szczęśliwy

Sad

Smutny

Angry

30 **Zły**

Scared

Przerażony

Frustration

Frustracja

Surprise

Niespodzianka

Shock

Szok

Brave

Odwaga

Baseball

Basketball

Baseball

Koszykówka

Tennis

Soccer

Tenis

Piłka nożna

Badminton

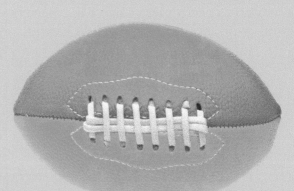

Badminton

Football

Futbol
amerykański

Volleyball

Siatkówka

Golf

Golf

Fire truck

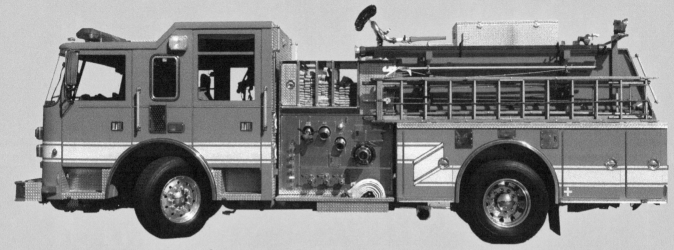

Wóz strażacki

Car

34 Samochód

Truck

Pickup

Helicopter

Helikopter

Airplane

Samolot

Train

Pociąg

Boat

Łódka

35

Small   Medium   Large

Mały   Średni   Duży

Small   Medium   Large

36 ## Mały   Średni   Duży

Large   Medium   Small

Duży   Średni   Mały

Large   Medium   Small

Duży   Średni   Mały   37

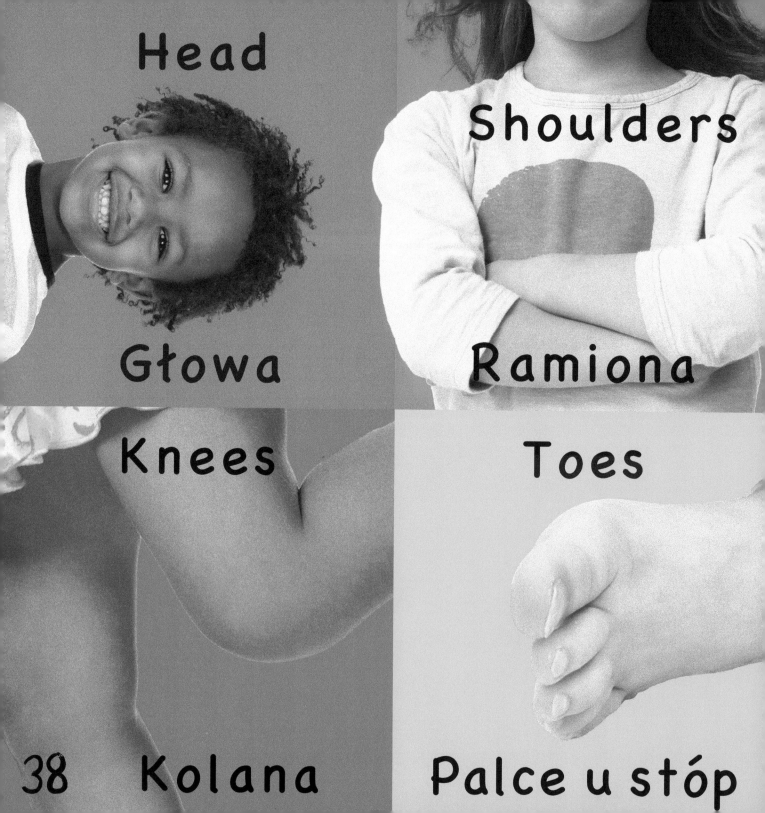

Head
Głowa

Shoulders
Ramiona

Knees
38 Kolana

Toes
Palce u stóp

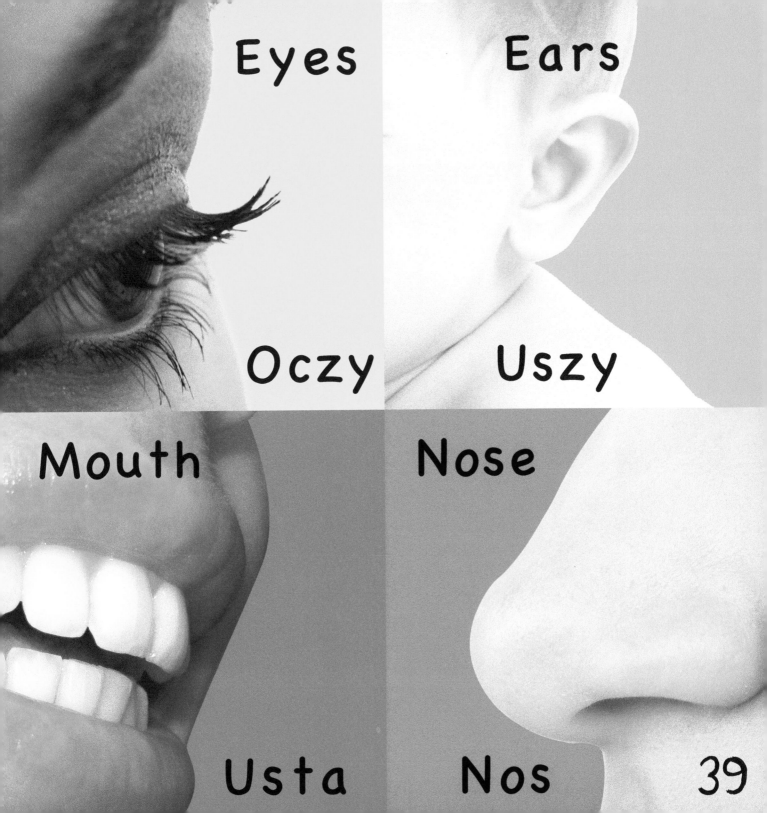

Eyes

Oczy

Ears

Uszy

Mouth

Usta

Nose

Nos

39

Sippy cup

Butelka dla dziecka

Bowl

Miska

Pot

Garnek

Cup

Kubek

40

Plate
Talerz

Fork
Widelec

Knife
Nóż

Spoon
Łyżka

Hat

Kapelusz

Shirt

Koszulka

Pants

42 Spodnie

Shorts

Spodenki

Gloves

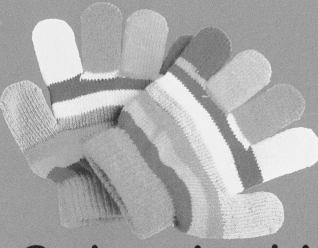

Rękawiczki

Sunglasses

Okulary
przeciwsłoneczne

Socks

Skarpetki

Shoes

Buty

43

Bath time
czas na kąpiel

Bath

Wanna

Soap

44 Mydło

Towel

Ręcznik

Brush

Myć zęby

Book

Książka

Potty

Nocnik

Bed

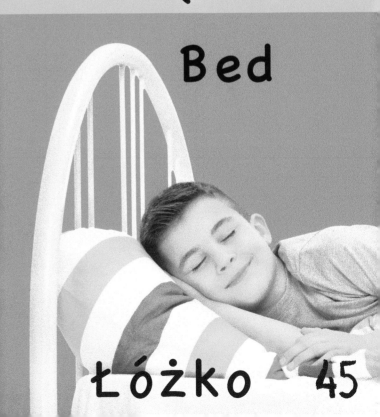

Łóżko 45

The Toddler's Handbook

activity / zadanie

Match the following to the pictures below. Can you find 7 pumpkins, a hooting owl, a rainbow, a baseball, a lion, square blocks, a sad boy, a helicopter, and shoes?

Poniżej przedstawiono zdjęcia. Czy możesz znaleźć 7 dyni, sowę, tęczę, baseball, lwa, kwadratowe bloki, smutnego chłopca, helikopter i buty?

helicopter / helikopter

shoes / buty

hooting owl / sowę

baseball / baseball

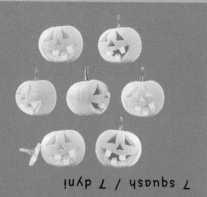

7 squash / 7 dyni

sad boy / smutny chłopiec

lion / lwa

square blocks / kwadratowe bloki

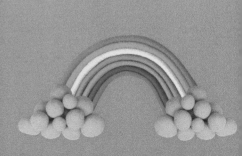

rainbow / tęczę

46

The Baby's handbook
With over 20 songs that every kid should know

DIDDLE · ITSY BITSY · TEA POT · TWINKLE · AIKEN DRUM · MUFFIN MAN · MACDONALD · MULBERRY · ROCK-A-BY · HICKORY · LITTLE LAMB · PAT-A-CAKE

The Preschooler's handbook
With over 300 Words that every kid should know

ABCs · NUMBERS · COLORS · SHAPES · MUSIC · SCHOOL · MANNERS · MATCHING · JOBS · ARTS · BRUSH TEETH · POTTY

The Kindergartener's handbook
With over 300 Words that every kid should know

ABCs · COLORS · MATH · SHAPES · VOWELS · TIME · SEASONS · SENSES · WEATHER · RHYMES · SCHOOL · CHORES

About the Author

Dayna Martin is the mother of three young boys. When she finished writing *The Toddler's Handbook* her oldest son was 18 months old, and she had newborn twins. Following the successful launch of her first book, Dayna began work on *The Baby's Handbook*, *The Preschooler's Handbook*, and *The Kindergartener's Handbook*. The ideas in her books were inspired by her search to find better ways to teach her children. The concepts were vetted by numerous educators in different grade levels. Dayna is a stay-at-home mom, and is passionate about teaching her children in innovative ways. Her experiences have inspired her to create resources to help other families. With thousands of copies sold, her books have already become a staple learning source for many children around the world.

Translations

ARABIC	JAPANESE
DUTCH	KOREAN
FILIPINO	MANDARIN
FRENCH	POLISH
GERMAN	PORTUGUESE
GREEK	RUSSIAN
HEBREW	SPANISH
HINDI	VIETNAMESE
ITALIAN	

Have comments or suggestions?
Contact us at: alexis@engagebooks.ca

Show us how you enjoy your **#handbook**. Tweet a picture to **@engagebooks** for a chance to win free prizes.

CPSIA information can be obtained
at www.ICGtesting.com
Printed in the USA
BVHW060040040121
596843BV00004B/287